Solstice and other Poems

Aurélia Lassaque

Solstice
and other
Poems

Poems in Occitan

Translated by James Thomas

First published by Francis Boutle Publishers
272 Alexandra Park Road
London N22 7BG
Tel/Fax: 020 8889 7744
Email: info@francisboutle.co.uk
www.francisboutle.co.uk

40269 c (12/12)

Solstice and Other Poems © Aurélia Lassaque 2012
Translations © James Thomas

ISBN 978 1903427 71 2

Printed by Melita Press, Malta

Acknowledgements

Some of the poems in *L'Alba dels Lops* (*Dawn of Wolves*) have appeared in their original Occitan and French versions in the following publications: *Cinquena Sason*, Toulouse, Letras d'òc, 2006; *Ombras de Luna – Ombres de Lune*, Nîmes, éd. de la Margeride, 2009-2010-2011; *E t'entornes pas – Et ne te retourne pas*, Nîmes, éd. de la Margeride, 2010; *Lo sòmi d'Euridícia – Le rêve d'Eurydice*, Frontignan, éd. les Aresquiers, 2011 ; *Lo sòmi d'Orfèu – Le rêve d'Orphée*, Frontignan, éd. les Aresquiers, 2011; two other poems were the fruit of a dialogue about poetry and painting with the Italian artist Adriana Civitarese and some have been the subject of artists' books produced by the American artist Julie Baugnet. Acknowledgements are due to these publishers and creative partners.

I want to thank James Thomas, an enigma ... James has captured, with remarkable accuracy, the subtleties, shades, contours and movements of a language and voice foreign to him. In our exchanges, we use three languages continuously. They cross, mingle and pursue one another, without debate or deliberation. Since day one, notwithstanding, we have basically spoken the same language, a language set free from the contingencies of temporality and the corporeality of borders.

I also thank Clive Boutle. At once I felt a strong affinity with this discoverer, his inquiring mind and his brilliant sense of humour. I will never forget how he had to excuse himself from another engagement so that he could attend my reading in the harsh London winter, where night suddenly encroaches on the bright afternoon.

James and Clive, together we lay a new stone in the foundation of "the walls of that city wherein the souls of the whole world may assemble" and give rise to the dream of the philosopher Romain Rolland ...

Aurélia Lassaque, June 2012

Translator's note: this quote is taken from C. K Ogden's 1916 translation of *Au-dessus de la mêlée* (*Above the Battle*) by Romain Rolland (1866-1944).

Contents

To my friend in prose
Boubacar Boris Diop

A note from the translator

It is a privilege and pleasure to produce translations for a living poet, especially when the poet works in a language not widely seen in English translation. Aurélia Lassaque (b. 1983) is a leading contemporary voice in Occitan, a language still thought erroneously by many to have died with the last troubadours of the late thirteenth century. Awareness of Occitan (and France's other historical languages) has increased markedly in recent years, though much of its literature is quite difficult to access outside southern France. Moreover, with some notable exceptions, contemporary Occitan literature is still largely a treasure chest awaiting future English translations. This volume, with its Occitan and English parallel texts, will introduce a rich poetic talent to a new readership and demonstrate the cultural dignity of modern Occitan.

Aurélia Lassaque is from near Albi in the Tarn *département*, north of Toulouse. Although she writes in Occitan, which she also speaks regularly, she has produced French 'versions' of every poem included here. Neither her Occitan nor French texts are 'translations' of each other; rather, both articulate a duality in her poetic vision. She engages in an original process of simultaneous bilingual creation where both languages cross paths repeatedly without merging into one.

Her poetry is characterised by a fascination with human interactions, emotions and the mysteries of the universe, a probing of the possibilities beyond the rituals and repetitions of time and the seasons. It is at once imagistic and metaphorical, sensual and compassionate. Imbued with the profoundly humanist spirit that characterizes what Simone Weil in a 1943 essay called 'Occitanian civilization' (*La civilization occitanienne*), it nonetheless escapes any simple attachment to *terroir* to embrace 'universal' themes long thought to be the preserve only of the national language.

In France, Aurélia Lassaque has published several bilingual Occitan-French volumes, won poetry prizes and coordinated conferences and exhibitions on the relationships between visual art and poetry. Translated into around ten languages and published in various reviews and anthologies, she has given readings throughout Europe and in Brazil. This is the first edition of her poetry to include full English translations and the first to be published in the United Kingdom. In addition to her most recent work *Solstice, the Call of Janus*, it includes nineteen other poems, most of which have been published already in their Occitan and French originals. Readers interested in the French versions of the poems should consult the bibliography in the acknowledgements.

I was introduced to Aurélia's poetry on Bastille Day, 2010 by Martin Sturge, a member of the Bath Royal Literary and Scientific Institution, who as part of a talk he was giving on Occitan and French poetry, asked me to read aloud one of her Occitan poems which he had translated into English. Martin is a long-standing friend of Aurélia and her family. I was struck by the concision, precision and delicacy of the poem; Martin kindly put me in touch with its author. Her response was enthusiastic and, after we met at her London reading in December 2011, Clive Boutle readily agreed to my proposal to translate and publish her new poem *Solstici* and a generous selection of other poems. I thank both Clive and Martin for enabling this project.

There are no set rules for translating poetry, yet myriad processes must be encountered and nurtured. My engagement with these poems is ongoing: the English translations are snapshots, albeit deeply-cogitated ones, of poems that are compelling in their imagery, rhythm, variety, allusiveness and, indeed, elusiveness. Although I relied for certain meanings on Aurélia's French versions, I have aimed at all times for poetic translations of the Occitan texts visible in this edition. I hope they capture the spirit of the originals.

James Thomas, Wiltshire, June 2012

Preface

It is timely and most welcome to have before us new Occitan writing made available to an English-language readership. It has been too easy to keep Occitan, language and literature, at the margins, and considered revivalist propaganda or nostalgia. But the zeitgeist is changing; Occitan should again have its place in the sun.

What the poetry of Aurélia Lassaque has let me rediscover is the excitement of hearing in my head the sounds of a lovely language which I scarcely know, but which nevertheless I find powerfully evocative and full of distant echoes. I have two good reasons for this. Firstly, I know Spanish (Castilian, that is) very well, and I had forgotten just how close to that language Occitan is. Secondly, my mother came from Auvergne, and my upbringing (albeit almost entirely in England) was accompanied by a kind of drip-feed of the Auvergnat dialect. Not, I confess, that I got to understand much of it. My mother never attempted to teach us it in any systematic way. Occasionally, she would put a record of Auvergnat *bourrées* on the turntable and start to translate the language of the sung pieces, but her desire to get dancing always got the better of her, and the lesson was quickly over. Besides, a bit naughtily, she and her sister reserved the dialect as their code for private conversations.

So today, savouring Aurélia Lassaque's poems, I find myself transported back to the French Midi, a living world of countryside and cities, most of it beautiful, some of it not, but predominantly a world of remembered scents and sounds. A world, too, rich in history. For many people, the lands where Occitan was used evoke troubadours, fortified castles, and the rest. But Aurélia Lassaque's poetic world is no museum of antiquities. Her poems, often small, always as polished as stones, are no exercises in history; they beat no drum for regionalism. The poet casts her gaze higher and wider than that; she confronts large and enduring issues as much as does 'mainstream' writing. The poems in this book are distillations of a human being's experience of living not just in one corner of one country, but on a planet which is vast, daunting, and sometimes frightening. Yes, the poet belongs to the 21st century, she lives deep in the south of France, and she has at her disposal a resilient and sonorously expressive language. That is her good fortune, but it is where she starts, not where she remains.

Her good fortune includes having James Thomas to translate her. Not only is James thoroughly at home in Occitan, he is a translator with a most sensitive touch. His accounts of the poems we have here attend most carefully to their Occitan originals, and become tactful and proportionate poems in their own right.

Here, then, is a volume of fine poetry in two languages, one familiar, the other less so. Now that attitudes are changing, and the Occitan world is gaining more attention, let us hope this book will encourage new audiences to discover that world. Thanks to Aurélia Lassaque, James Thomas, and Clive Boutle, the publisher, I am certain it will.

Martin Sorrell
Emeritus Professor of French,
Exeter University

Solstici

Lo bram de Janus

Solstice

The Call of Janus

Sant-Joan

Lo Jorn

St John's Eve

Day

La granja quilhada a la termièra de las sasons liura sa flaira de bauca cauda.

Los cavals joves trepejan e se fan la guèrra pel plaser de mesclar la susor de lors còsses al tast del primièr sang.

The barn standing at the seasons' border
releases sweet aromas of cut grass.

Young horses tramp hooves in a war dance
savouring the sweaty mesh of bodies
tasting first blood.

Dins los ostals de las tampas clausas,
la fusta carrinca
e se confla d'impaciéncia.

Los òmes, entre òmes, retròban lor natura.

Se copa lo vin amb de glacets
per enganar la clardat del jorn
calhat coma un tombèl dins l'èrm.

Inside closely-shuttered houses,
wood restlessly
swells and creaks.

Men amongst men embrace their nature.

Wine watered with ice cubes
deceives the daylight
fixed like a tomb in the desert.

Lo solelh al zenit embeu l'anar de la mainada enferonida.

The zenith sun soaks up the scurry of suddenly-wild children.

Es arribada de las Americas
ambe lo tren,
ambe la mar,
ambe l'estieu
e sas valisas lusentas.

Dins sos pelses, una belaròia qu'agafa de parpalhòls d'aur.

Sas cilhas pausadas coma un vel sus sos uèlhs de fuòc.

She's come from the Americas
by train,
by sea,
with summer
and her glistening cases.

A gemstone in her hair catches golden butterflies.

Her lashes poised like a veil over eyes of fire.

Lo lenhièr
immense
tuteja lo cèl
e la mòrt que se sarra.

The colossal
stake
caresses the sky
and oncoming death.

Dins d'ostals sornes
los vièlhs,
las femnas
e los relòtges
fan mina de dormir.

An lo morre badièr
e d'uèlhs d'aucèls mòrts.

Inside sombre houses
the elders,
women
and clocks
feign sleeping faces.

Mouths gaping open,
eyes like dead birds'.

La bèla se banha.

La ribièra a cambiat de lièch
e contra son còs liurat
l'aiga negra a sortit sos tambors
per que canten las blandas.

Bella's bathing.

The river's changed course;
against her given body
dark waters beat their drums
to salamanders singing.

Los ausidors brandan al pè del lenhièr,
la sang perleja suls còsses
e l'alen se fa brusent.

Las campanas estabosidas
esquinçan l'aire en suspens
quand lo ser enaiga las carrièras.

Below the stake eardrums burn,
blood seeps from bodies,
breath reverberates.

Dumbfounded, the bells
cleave hanging air as
evening floods the streets.

Sant-Joan

Lo Ser

Saint John's Eve

Evening

La bèla a liurat sos pelses als dets de l'èrba.

Dins l'insoléncia del calabrun
los pibols fan dançar lor ombra
contra sa pèl de fuòc.

Bella's hair unfurls between fingers of grass.

Under twilight's brazen glare
poplar-tree shadows dance
around her skin of fire.

Las femnas son sarradas contra lors òmes,
los dròlles contra lors maires
e las sòrres targan lors fraires.

Lo cec jòga de violon
coma un capitani bandat
que semena la tempèsta.

Women cling closely to their men,
children to their mothers,
– sisters probe their brothers.

The blind man plays violin
like a drunken captain
sowing the storm.

Sota las taulas e los bancs garrèls,
los dròlles jògan a la faula dels primièrs òmes…

Under rickety chairs and tables,
children play at fables of first men…

S'es endormida, la bèla,
breçada pel moviment de la darrièra lutz
sus sas longas parpèlas.

Contra son esquina,
la freula ronda de la terra
e las pèiras que velhan dedins.

Bella's sleeping now,
cradled by last light's fading cadence
on her long eyelids.

Skating against her back,
the delicate dance of earth
and sleeping stones within.

La brisa ardenta abraça la taulejada
e pausa sus las labras mostosas
un perfum de darrièr jorn del monde.

An eager breeze embraces the evening feast,
sprinkling onto moistened lips
a last-day-of-the-world perfume.

Los dròlles se liuran a de juòcs primitius dins las cavas.

Children inside caves engage in primitive games.

De cosin a cosina, los agaches s'atardivan.

De braces perduts fregan d'ancas languivas.

Las voses se fan prigondas e la sang arrasa sota la pèl.

Gazes linger lazily between cousins.

Straying arms brush against languorous hips.

As voices are lowered, blood quickens beneath the skin.

Los ancians braman qu'es ora del grand fuòc.

Prudentas,
las canturlas desaparèissan dins las flambas
en marmolhar qualque pregària.

The elders bellow time for the great fire.

Murmuring prayers,
old maids proceed warily
into the flames.

Sant-Joan

La Nuèch

St John's Eve

Night

La bèla bala sola suls camins
per las estèlas e per la salvatgina,
sas mans penjadas al cèl,
daissa lo vent la vesitar.

Son rire se mescla al cant d'aucèls de nuèch allucinats.

Bella dances alone down paths
of watching stars and waterfowl;
with hands hanging from the sky,
she welcomes the calling wind.

Her laughter melds with the sounds of tripped-out night birds.

Lo fuòc esquinça los bombets.

Ronda de còsses en fusion per un balèti d'instruments mòrts.

Bodices ripped by fire.

Bodies melting in the round mime a ballet of dead instruments.

Dins los camps
las regas se cavan
per aculhir lo galòp del bestial fugidís.

Thickening furrows
in fields extend their welcome
for a herd on the run.

Esfinxes desfisant l'azur,
las ègas an desligada lor crinièra d'alabastre
e empòrtan dins lor fugida
lo Camin de Sant-Jaume.

Sphinxes scorning the skies,
the mares unleash their manes of alabaster;
in milky flight
they steal away the Heavens.

Jaguda sus la tèrra estrementida,
la bèla sospira
quand limpan sus son còs alandat
de sèrps lubrics.

En garbas, amolonadas,
las nivols curiosas esperlongan la nuèch,
quand de sa boca s'escapa un raufèl sublim
que descabestra lo fólzer.

Spread-eagled on trembling earth,
Bella sighs;
over her outstretched body
lustful snakes slide.

Stacked-up, in wreath-like banks,
curious clouds drag out the darkness;
from her mouth a sublime moan
roams and rouses thunderbolts.

Lo bestial se retròba al temps qu'èra joine
e mèstre de sa natura,
al temps que parlava als rius e al vent
e que cantava la gèsta dels arbres
a las flors salvatjas meravilhadas.

The herd turns back to when it was young,
master of its nature;
to when it spoke with the wind and streams
and sang of the trees' epic deeds
to flowers wild with wonder.

Lo tròn ronca
coma un rire de titan
que talhvira las armas,
escrifa los teissuts,
e desliura los còsses.

Lo brandal es emmascat
per sos quites rebats
dins lo juòc dels còsses mesclats.

La luna udola naut dins lo cèl
e son crit
se pèrd dins la boca badanta del brasàs.

Thunder rumbles
like titanic laughter
corroding souls,
tearing tissue,
unbinding bodies.

The great flame fizzes, bewitched
by its own shimmering
in the play of mingling skins.

The moon howls high in the sky;
its cry fades
into the flagrant mouth of the inferno.

Prima Alba d'Estieu

First Summer Dawn

Es tornada per las Americas
dins las cendres
amb l'auròra
amb la pluèja
lo silenci
e sas valisas lusentas.

She's gone back to the Americas
in the embers
with the dawn
with the rain
silence
and her glistening cases.

Dins sos pelses de flors de nuèch aconsomidas.

Night flowers lie sleeping in her hair.

Dins los ostals de las tampas dubèrtas,
los esposes dormisson coma al primièr jorn.

Dieuses de cendre
perduts dins la carn de lors pantaises.

Inside open-shuttered houses,
couples sleep as on the first day.

Gods of cinder
lost in the flesh of their fantasies.

L'Alba dels Lops

Divèrses Poèmas

Dawn of Wolves

Various poems

Pantais

Fai freg dins mon anma
Es romantic e desuet.
Ieu
Auriái presa la nau en Grècia.
A Santorin auriái limpat
Sus l'esquina d'un ase
Fins a la mar.
Auriái penjat mon lum
A la branca d'un olivièr.
E dins un ostal blanc
Auriái aimat de pescaires esperitals
E de monges desfrocats.

Fantasy

My soul is cold inside;
It's quaint, romantic.
Me,
I would have boarded the boat in Greece.
At Santorini I'd have drifted
On the back of a mule
Right out to sea.
I would have hung up my light
On the branch of an olive tree.
Inside a whitewashed house
I'd have made love to divine fishermen
And defrocked monks.

Indecéncia

Es arribat
Los lops an manjada la posca.
Dins lors cròsses
Las trenèlas de las canturlas
Se son desligadas.
Los borrilhs de mai
An denudada la pibola.
Los obrièrs
S'evasisson
Dins de pantaisses
De pèira seca
E de filhas brunas.

Fai rotge
Sus las nòstras caras.

Indecency

It's done:
Wolves have devoured the dust.
Inside their vaults
Old maids' plaits
Slacken and unbraid.
May's gossamer flakes
Have stripped the aspen bare.
Workers
Break free
Into fantasies
Of dry stone
And dark-haired girls.

Blushes paint
Our faces red.

Crimi

La tampa tustava
Contra la paret,
Era sola
Al dedins de l'ostal
Per velhar prèp del mòrt
Dins sa cambra a ela.
Sola amb el
Sa paur
E sos joguets
Escampats pel sòl.
Se diguèt que lo velhariá
Fins a l'alba
Puèi que li fariá una tomba
Amb un entarrament,
Al lausèrt qu'aviá tuat.

Crime

The shutter clatterered
Against the wall;
She was alone
Inside the house,
In her room keeping watch
Over the dead body.
Alone with it,
Her fear
And her toys
Scattered on the floor.
She thought she'd guard it
Until dawn –
Then she'd make a grave
In which to bury
The lizard she'd killed.

Dins una mar luenchenca,
Perdut entre doas guèrras,
Lo vièlh soldat cerca
Dins l'escuma que salunha de la nau,
Son caval e son espasa,
Sos sòmis de cort d'escòla.

Sas lagrèmas,
Aquí ont son tombadas,
Se son cambiadas en pèrlas.

On a far distant sea,
Lost between two wars,
The old soldier tries to find
Amidst the ship's spuming foam
His horse and his sword,
His playground daydreams.

His teardrops,
In the spaces where they fell,
Have turned into pearls.

Lo fraire de Jacmelina

Lo fraire de Jacmelina
Aviá perdut las dents puèi lo cap.
Sietat a l'ombra manèla d'un telh
Esperava sa paura maire
Coma un drollet plan ensenhat.
Los cats, lor disiá « Bonsoir messieurs ».
Los autres ne risián pas qu'amassa
E boca clavada
Per mostrar pas que lor dents tanben
Se degalhavan.

Al Paradís
Entrepreses e paurucs
Lo retrobèron a la drecha de Sant Pèire.

Un cat sietat sus sa tèsta lor diguèt
« Bienvenu messieurs ».

Jacqueline's brother

Jacqueline's brother
Had lost his teeth and then his mind.
Sitting in a lime-tree's tranquil shade
He'd wait for his poor mother
Like a well-bred schoolboy.
To cats he'd say "Good Evening, Sirs".
The others only laughed at him in gangs
With mouths shut tight
To hide the rotten stench of
Their own teeth.

In Paradise
Perplexed and full of fear
They found him to the right of Saint Peter.

A cat seated upon his head greeted them:
"Welcome, Gentlemen."

Apocalipsi

Lo cèl aquela nuèch
Aviá manjada la luna.
L'òme aimava
Lo còs de sa femna.
Lo dròlle jogava a la bala
Contra la paret.
I a pas que la vièlha
E lo can
Que comprenguèron
Aquela nuèch
Que la fin èra pròche.

Demorèron muts.

Apocalypse

The sky, that night,
Had swallowed the moon.
A man delighted
In his wife's body.
A child bobbed and bounced a ball
Against the wall.
On that night
Only the old woman
And the dog
Understood
That the end was nigh.

They remained silent.

De sa maire beguèt lo lach,
De sa femna manjèt la carn,
De sos dròlles cremèt los cervèls,
Pr'aquò compren pas sa solesa.
Son ostal bèu la pluèja,
Sa terra engolís las pèiras.
Demorarà lo rei de l'istòria que conta,
Es lo privilègi dels mostres d'aiçaval.

He drank the milk of his mother,
He ate the flesh of his wife
And burned the brains of his children;
Yet he can't fathom his feeling alone.
His house laps up the rain,
His land gorges on stones.
He'll always be king in the story he tells,
That's the privilege of monsters here below.

Lo temps s'es perdut
Dins los camins de l'èr
Ont, ausèl sens còs,
Una cara de dròlla
Pren sa volada.
Una perla negra dins sos uèlhs
S'escapa cap al cèl d'Icara.
Es filha del neient
Que li daissèt en eritatge
Un tròç de nuèch sens luna
Sus las labras.
Jamai tocarà tèrra
Jamai tutejarà la pèira
Nimai los arbres
E l'aiga que los enjaura,
Qu'a esposada una quimèra
Que se perdèt dins lo vent.

Time has disappeared
Into the air-tracks
Where a young girl's face,
Bird without body,
Takes flight.
From her eyes a black pearl
Escapes to Icaria sky.
She's daughter to oblivion
That bequeathed her
A morsel of moonless night,
Left on her lips.
She'll never touch earth
She'll never tease the stone
Nor the trees
Nor the waters that confound them.
She married an illusion
That vanished in the wind.

Dins sa rauba de nuèch
La mar a cordurat
Una cara aconsomida

Una serena curiosa
La vòl per ela sola
E bala dins l'onda suauda
Amb aquela que la mar empòrta
Dins las prigondors de son cant.

Inside her night dress
The sea has sewn
A face that is sleeping

A mermaid, curious,
Wants it for herself
And dances in the serene waters
With the one whom the sea sweeps
Into the depths of her song.

Lo rei de seda saura

Engana l'aucelum e tuteja l'aura.
Quilhat dins l'èrba salvatja
A perdut sos uèlhs
Raubats a la vèsta d'un soldat.
Tres gojats son venguts
Qu'an escampat sas tripas pel sòl
Per i prene qualque dròlla mal pintrada.

Privat de son còs de seda saura,
L'espaurugal
Fa de sòmis descabestrats
Que desvarian los aucèls.

The king of golden silk

He ensnares birds and banters with the wind.
Pitched on wild grassland
He's lost his eyes
Stolen from the coat of a soldier.
Three young lads came along
Scattered his guts on the ground
Where they laid a dishevelled girl.

Without his body of golden silk
The scarecrow
Dreams ungovernable dreams
That bewilder the birds.

Sa pèl escura e cauda
Coma una nuèch d'estieu
S'estira fins a fintar l'alba
Quand son còs de cavala fèra
Tornamai s'alanda
E cava dins la prigondor de sas cambas
Un paradís d'auselaire.

Her skin, hot and dark
Like a summer's night,
Stretches to catch out the dawn
As her wild-mare body moves,
Uncoiling once more
Probing in the deepness of her limbs
A bird-catcher's paradise.

Passava en secret d'oradas dins lo verdièr
Pausant sa lenga contra la saba rossa
Gotejant de las bocas badantas dels arbres.
Aital, un ser d'auratge joven,
La trobèt un gojat vengut de la mar
Que l'emportèt a la cima de son sèxe.

She spent long secret hours in the orchard
Resting her tongue against russet sap
Seeping from the trees' gaping mouths;
One evening of gathering storms,
A young man from the sea found her
And stole her away on his carnal crown.

La negressa somiava
D'iranges roges e redondes,
Miralh vegetal
De sas popas regolejantas de lach nòu;
Li nasquèt un dròlle
Del pel rosset e dels uèlhs verds
Que servava en secret
Dins una banasta de fruchas falsas.

A black woman dreamed
Of round, red oranges,
A pulpy mirror
Of her breasts, dripping new milk;
She bore a boy
With russet hair and green eyes;
In secret she kept him
In a basket of false fruits.

An viatjat tras los matins verds
Subre las aigas de l'ailà,
An virat tantes còps dins los cèls clars,
An saludadas las milantas mòrts dels astres
E son tornats als camps paures
Per centenas
Dins l'amudiment del temps present,
Los aucèls del cande matin.

Beyond green mornings they glided
Over other-worldly waters,
So many times they circled the clearest skies,
Greeted the infinite last gasps of the stars
And returned to meagre fields
In their hundreds
In the muteness of present time,
Birds of pure morning.

Un ostal de pèira e de cortinas de lin
coloradas per la lutz e la posca mescladas.
La mar granda, fins a l'asuèlh,
agacha per la fenèstra.
Dins l'ostal, una femna encara verge;
sos pelses de cendre qu'atissa lo vent de la nauta mar
balan amb lo ser.
Sus la taula,
son vièlh trocèl ben plegat,
atrai son agach
quand los aucèls de nuech se mèton a cantar.

A house of stone and linen curtains
tinted by rays of light and dust.
The ocean, stretching to the horizon,
peers through the window.
Inside the house, a virginal woman;
her ashen hair, teased by winds from the high seas,
dances with the evening.
On the table,
her old, well-folded trousseau
catches her eye
just as the night birds start to sing.

A l'ora del solstici
Lo pòble vestit de fusta
Atraisa dins sa rama
D'aucèls sens cara.

Lo riu barrutlaire
Carreja dusca als ribals
Sos remembres de nèu.

Los aubres de ma selva
An rogejat al primièr jorn de l'estieu.

Los òmes de la vila
An dich qu'aquò's la rovilha
E que ven del Japon.

Mas eles sabon pas
Que los aubres d'aquela comba
Dins lo secret de lors rasigas
Alisan de pèiras vivas
Que se mèton a somiar
Que l'aura e la pluèja
Las prendràn nusas sul bard
A l'ora del solstici.

At the solstice hour
People dressed in wood
Lure into their leafage
Birds without faces.

The wandering stream
Drags towards the shores
Its memories of snow.

My sylvan trees
Have reddened with summer's first day.

The men from the town
Said that was rust
Blown in from Japan.

But they don't know
That the trees in this coomb
In their deepest secret roots
Stroke living stones
That start to dream
That the wind and the rain
Will take them naked on clay
At the solstice hour.

As pres lo camin del país de nuèch.
Lo desèrt i es de gèl
E las estèlas se languisson.
Obris tos braces e cava,
La posca serà ton pan,
T'abeuraràn nòstras lagremas.
Vai, vai e t'entornes pas.
S'ausisses udolar la pèira,
Es que s'i gravan las letras de ton nom.

You've chosen the path for the land of night.
The desert is made of ice there
And the stars die of boredom.
Stretch out your arms and dig,
Dust will be your bread,
You'll swallow our tears.
Go now, go, and don't return.
If you hear the stones wailing,
The letters of your name are being engraved.

Lo sòmi d'Orfeù

Dins los infèrns que los òmes
Son pas mai que d'ombras.
Me farai ombra al dedins de ton còs.

Bastirai de ciutats de sabla
Qu'agotaràn lo flum que degun ne tòrna.

Dansarem sus de torres que nòstres uèlhs veiràn pas.

Serai ta lenga trencada que sap pas mentir.

E maudirem l'amor que nos a perduts.

The Dream of Orpheus

In the Underworld, where men
Are nothing more than shades,
I'll shadow myself within your body.

I'll fashion cities of sand
That bleed dry the river of no return.

We'll dance upon towers that our eyes cannot see.

I'll be your severed tongue that tells no lies.

And we'll curse the love that lost us.

Lo sòmi d'Euridícia

Cavarem d'autras regas que cobrirem de cendre.
Veirem morir lo vent carrejaire d'oblit.
Aurai de pomas dins ma pòcha raubadas a mai paure
que ieu.
Las pelarem amb d'espasas.
E amb çò que sòbra de nòstres sòmis
Ne bastirem mai
Delà los fuòcs
E la termièra de l'agach.

The Dream of Euridice

We'll dig other furrows and fill them with ash.
We'll see dying the carrier-wind of oblivion.
In my pocket I'll carry apples stolen from poorer souls
than me.
We'll peel them with sabres.
With what's left of our dreams
We'll fashion others
Beyond the fires
And frontiers of our eyes.